1

SECOND EDITION

LET'S GO

Student Book

Ritsuko Nakata
Karen Frazier
Barbara Hoskins
Steve Wilkinson

with songs by Carolyn Graham

Oxford University Press
198 Madison Avenue, New York, NY 10016, USA
Great Clarendon Street, Oxford OX2 6DP, England

Oxford New York
Auckland Bangkok Buenos Aires Cape Town Chennai
Dar es Salaam Delhi Hong Kong Istanbul Karachi Kolkata
Kuala Lumpur Madrid Melbourne Mexico City Mumbai Nairobi
São Paulo Shanghai Taipei Tokyo Toronto

OXFORD is a trademark of Oxford University Press.

ISBN 0-19-436443-7

Editorial Manager: Shelagh Speers
Senior Editor: Sherri Arbogast
Editor: Lynne Robertson
Editorial Assistant: Christine Hartzler
Production Editor: Mark Steven Long
Elementary Design Manager: Doris Chen Pinzon
Designer: Ruby Harn
Senior Art Buyers: Alex Rockafellar, Patricia Marx
Production Manager: Shanta Persaud

Printing (last digit): 10 9 8
Printed in China.

***Original character art by* Dora Leder.**
***Characters rendered by* Dora Leder, Bill Colrus, Mena Dolobowsky, *and* Michael Ng.**
Other illustrations by Yvette Banek, Shirley Beckes/Craven Design, Rusty Fletcher, Patrick Girouard, Steve Henry, Sharon Holm, Anne Kennedy, Tammie Lyon, Paul Meisel, Patrick Merrell, Maggie Swanson, and Jim Talbot

Cover design by Doris Chen Pinzon/Ruby Harn
Cover production by Ogdemli/Feldman Design, Inc.
Cover illustration by Bill Colrus

To our editors at Oxford University Press, and to the design team, thank you for your inspiration and hard work. To our husbands and children, thank you for your support and understanding. We would like to dedicate this series to the Wilkinson family in loving memory of Steve Wilkinson, our colleague and friend.

Icons

Let's Go Student Book 1 consists of eight units, with a review section after every two units. Every unit is divided into six lessons. Each lesson is identified by a colorful icon. The same icons are used for reference on the corresponding pages in both the *Workbook* and the *Teacher's Book*.

Let's Talk
Functional dialogue

Let's Sing
Interactive song based on the dialogue

Let's Learn
New grammatical structure

Let's Learn Some More
Related grammatical structure

Let's Move
Classroom commands and action verbs

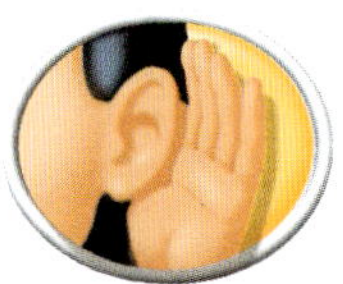

Let's Listen
Listening test and unit review

Let's Review
Further review after every two units

Table of Contents

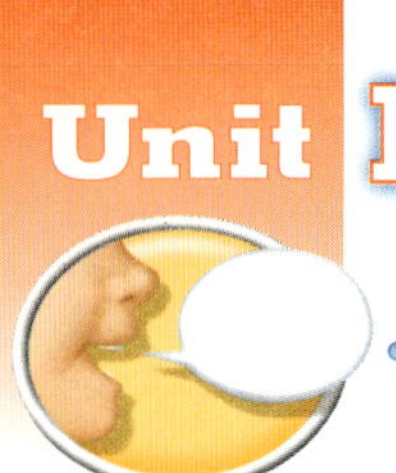

Unit 1

Let's Talk

What is your name?
My name is John.

What is = What's

Let's Sing

Jenny

Lisa

Andy

Scott

The Hello Song

Hello, hello, hello!
What's your name?
Hello, hello, hello!

My name is John.
My name is John.

Hello, John!
Hello, John!
Hello!

Kate

John

Let's Learn

What is this?
It is a ruler.

What is = What's
It is = It's

Practice.

What's this?
It's a book.
1. a book
2. a desk
3. a chair
4. a ruler
5. a pencil
6. a bag
7. a pen
8. an eraser

Let's Learn Some More

Is this a book?
Yes, it is.
No, it is not.

is not = isn't

Practice.

Is this a pen?

No, it isn't. It's a pencil.

1. 

2. 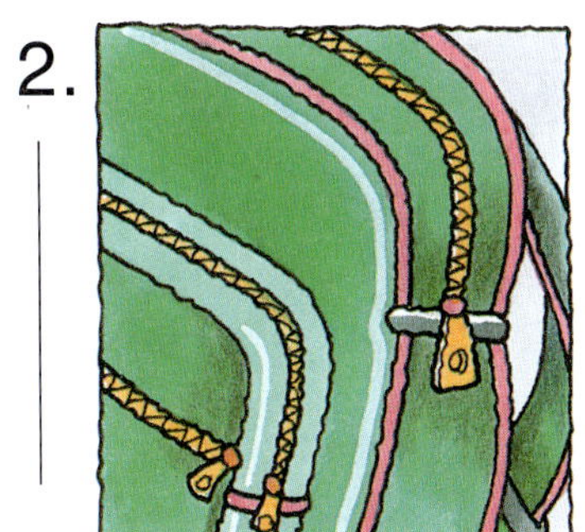

3. 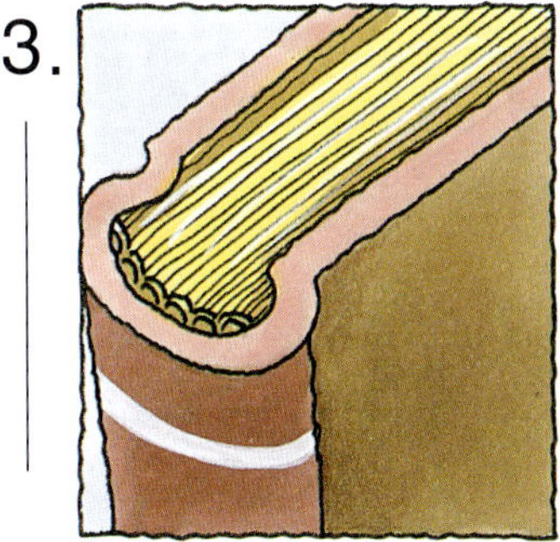

4. 

5. 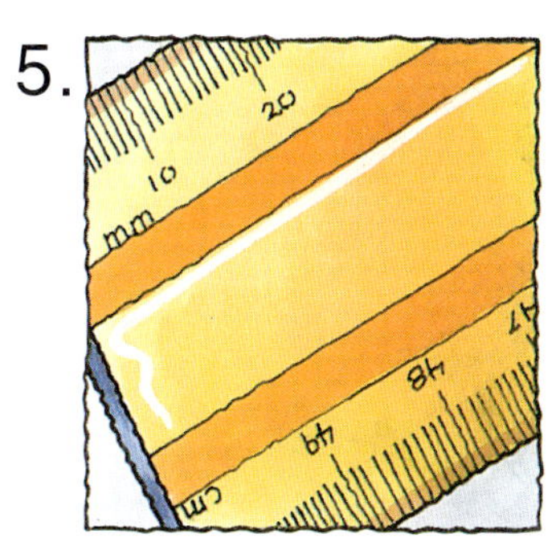

6. 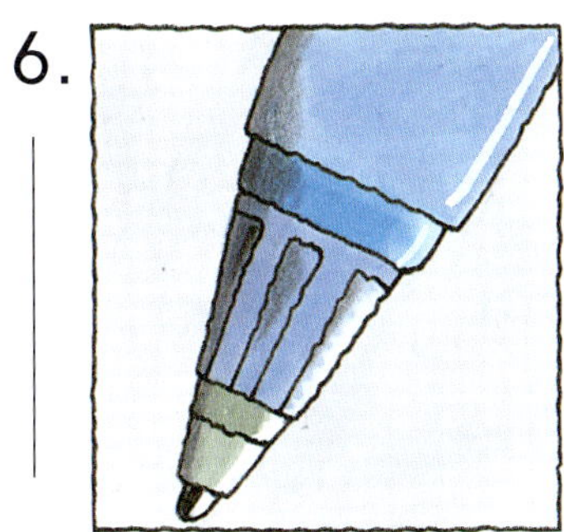

7. 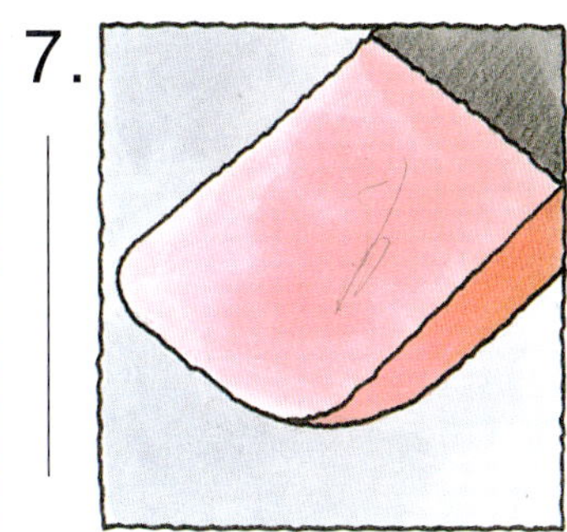

8. 

Learn the alphabet.

I like English!

♪ The Alphabet Song ♪

A B C D E F G H
I J K L M N O
P Q R S T U V W X Y Z

Let's Move

1. Stand up.

2. Sit down.

3. Open your book.

4. Close your book.

5. Point to the teacher.

6. Touch your desk.

7. Please be quiet.

8. Listen carefully.

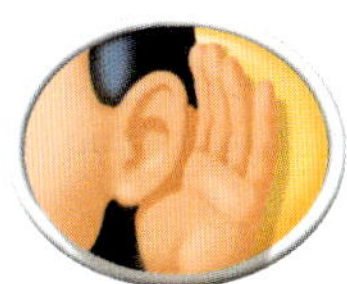

Let's Listen

1.

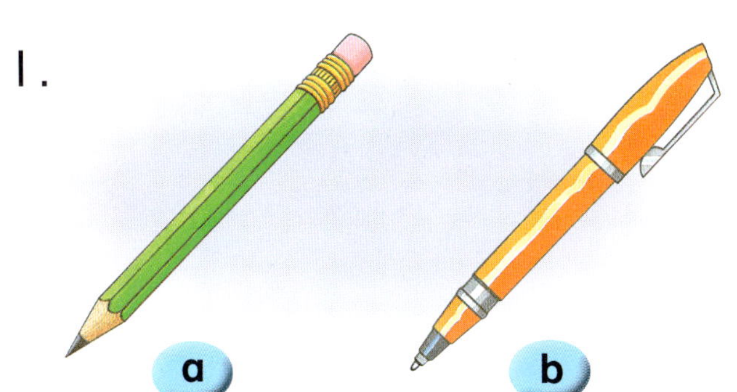

2.

3.

4.

5.

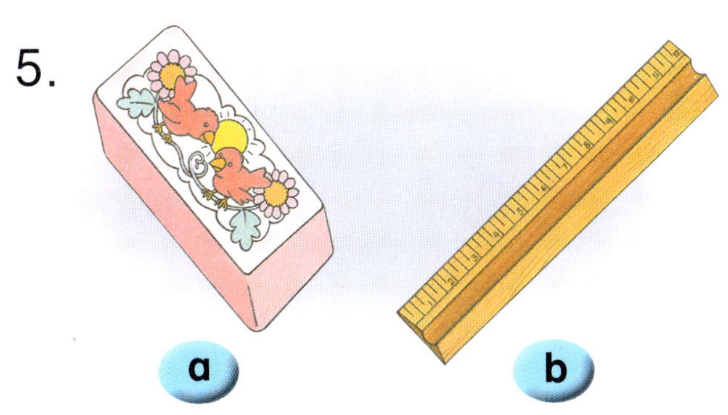

6.

7.

8.

Unit 2

Let's Talk

Hi, Andy. How are you?

I'm fine.
How are you?

I'm fine. Thank you.

How are you?
I am fine. Thank you.

I am = I'm

Let's Sing

Hi, How Are You?

Hi, how are you?
I'm fine.
Hi, how are you?
I'm fine.
Hi, how are you?
I'm fine. How are you?
I'm fine, I'm fine, I'm fine.

Let's Learn

What color is this?

It's red!

What color is this?
It is red.

It is = It's

1. yellow

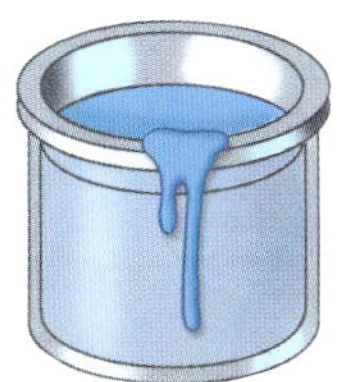
2. blue

3. white

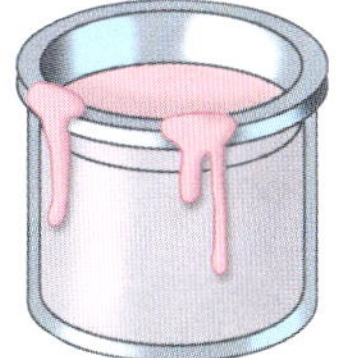
4. pink

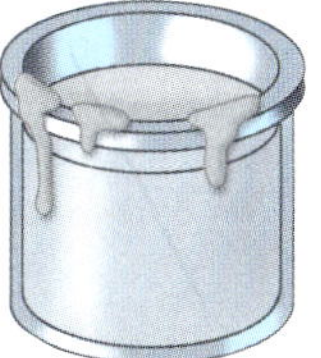
5. gray

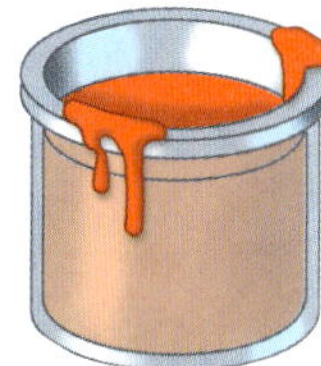
6. red

7. black

8. green

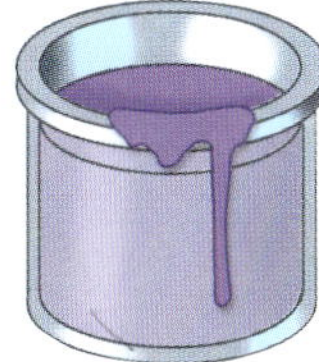
9. purple

10. orange

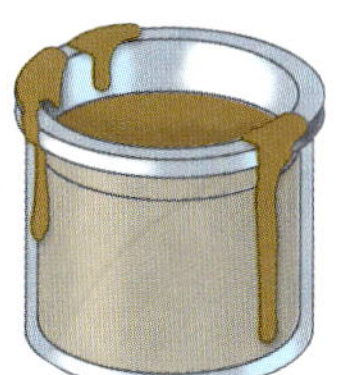
11. brown

♪ The Black Cat Song ♪

Green grass, blue skies,
Black cats, yellow eyes,
Red birds, blue skies,
Black cats, yellow eyes.

White clouds, blue skies,
Black cats, yellow eyes,
Black cats, blue skies,
Yellow, yellow eyes.

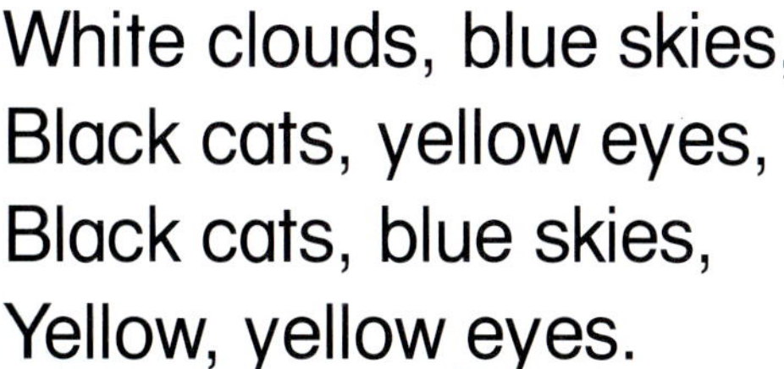

Let's Learn Some More

This is a blue book.
This is a red and yellow book.

1.

2.

3.

4.

5.

6.

7.

8.

Learn the alphabet.

a b c d e f g h i j k l m n o p q r s t u v w x y z

A a

apple

B b

book

C c

cat

Let's Move

1. Raise your hand.

2. Put your hand down.

3. Take out your book.

4. Put your book away.

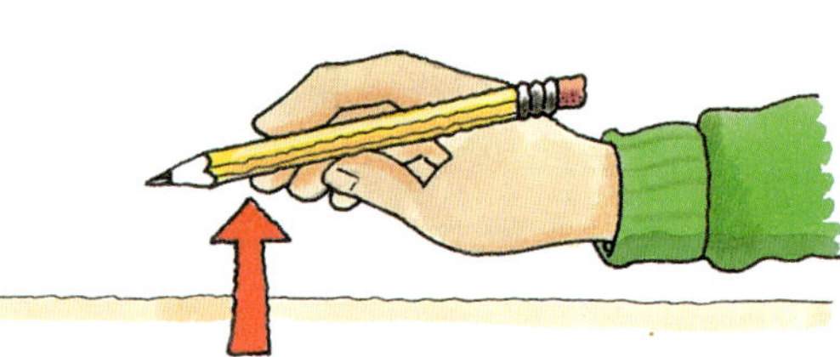

5. Pick up your pencil.

6. Put your pencil down.

7. Write your name.

8. Look at the board.

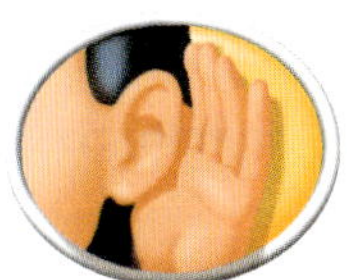

Let's Listen

1.

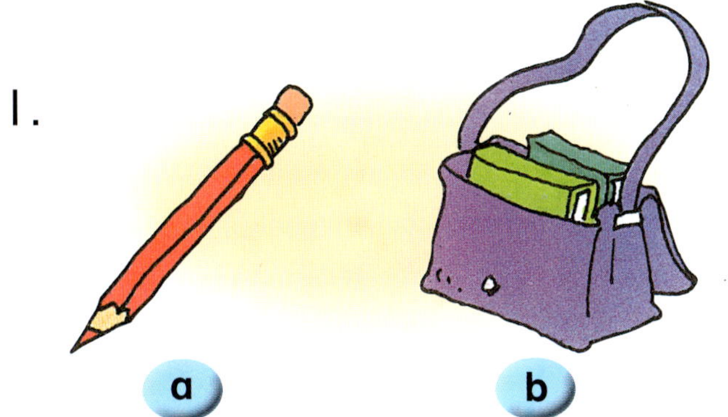

a b

2.

a b

3.

a b

4.

a b

5.

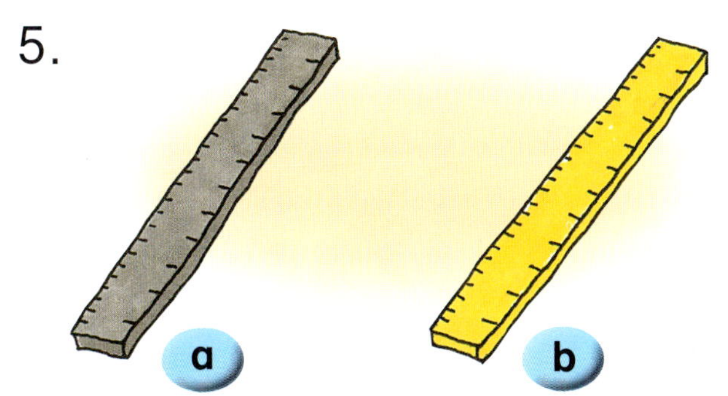

a b

6.

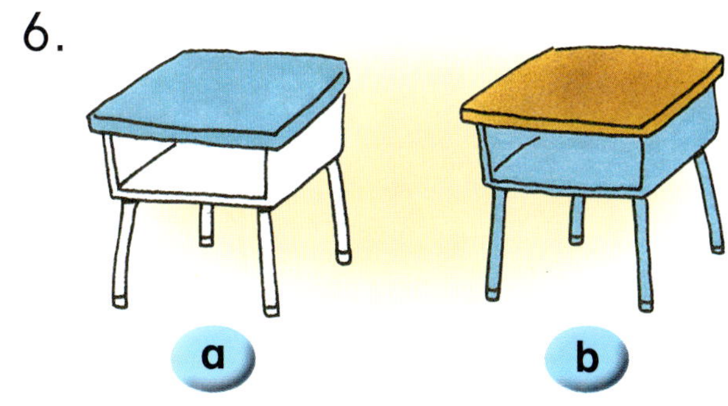

a b

7.

a b

8.

a b

Let's Review

A. Play a game.

What's this?

It's a pink pencil.

CATS

START

END

B. Say and act.

C. Ask your partner.

Is this a _______?

1. 
2. 
3. 
4. 
5. 
6. 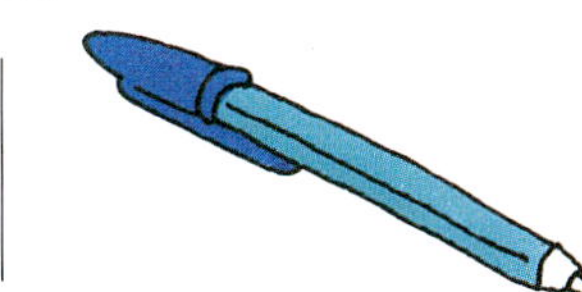
7. 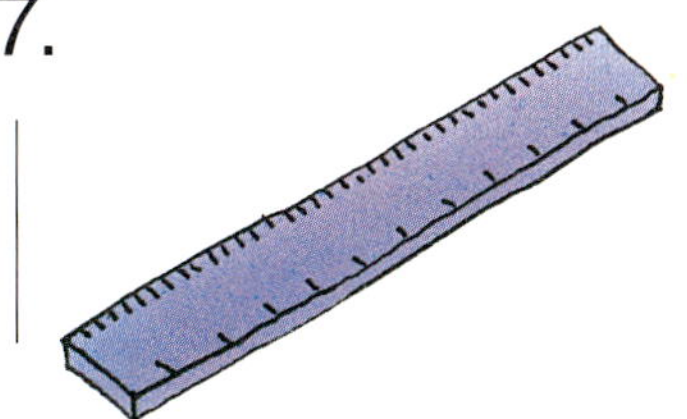
8. 

D. Listen carefully.

1. 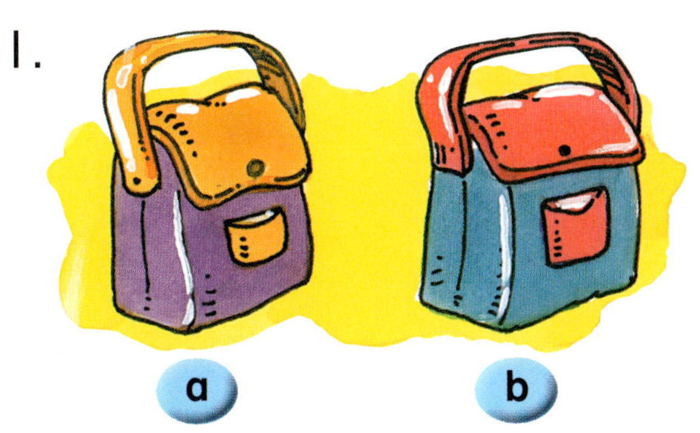

a b

2. 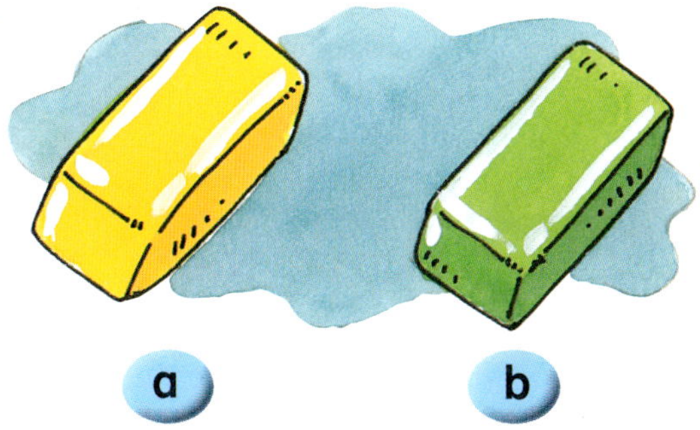

a b

Let's Talk

Hi, John.
This is my friend, Sarah.

Hello, Sarah.

Hi, John.

Let's play!

This is my friend, Sarah.
Hello, Sarah.

Let's Sing

This Is My Friend

This is my friend, Sarah.
Hello, Sarah.
This is my friend, Sarah.
Hello, Sarah.

This is my friend, John.
Hi, John!
This is my friend, John.
Hi, John!

This is my friend, Sarah.
This is my friend, John.
Let's play!

Let's Learn

What are these?
They are cassettes.

They are = They're

Practice.

What's this?

It's a crayon.
What are these?

They're crayons.

1. 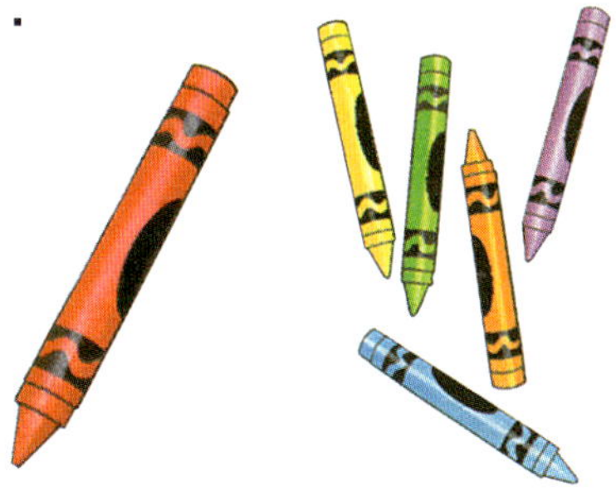 a crayon — crayons
2. a pencil case — pencil cases
3. a table — tables
4. a cassette — cassettes
5. a marker — markers
6. a notebook — notebooks

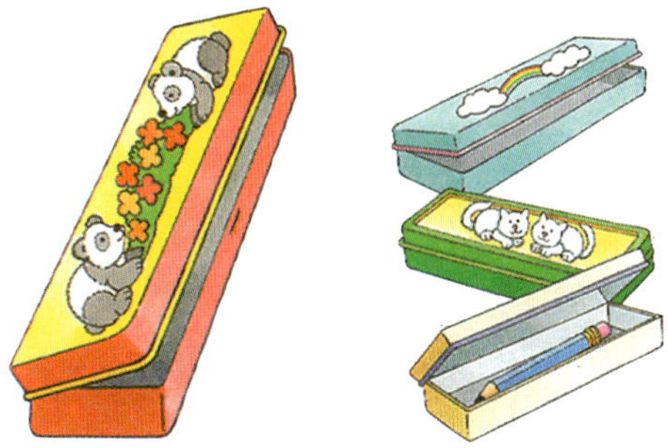

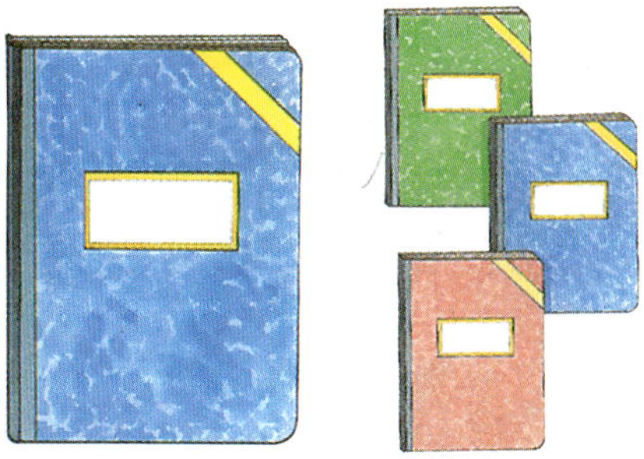

Say these.

This is a ______. These are ______.

Let's Learn Some More

The Purple Sneaker Song

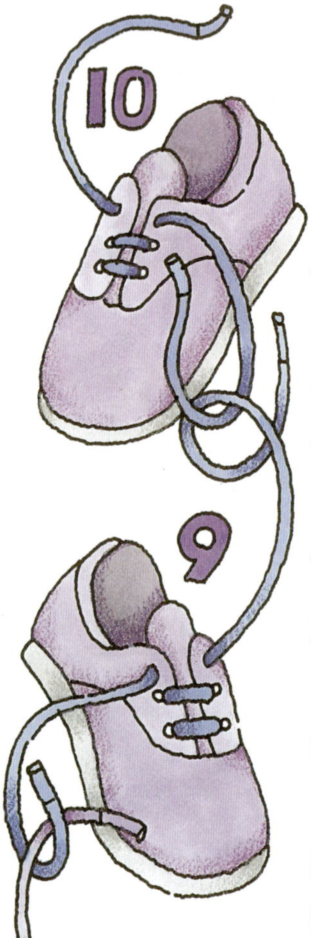

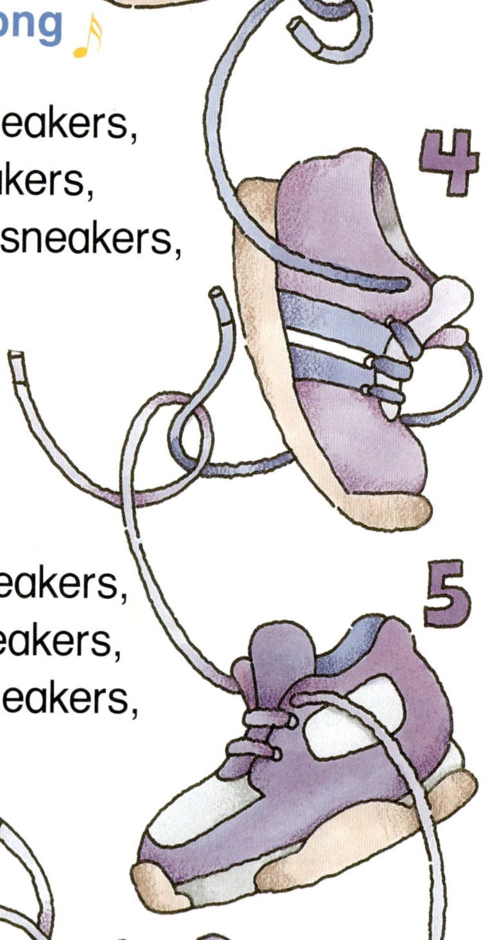

One little, two little, three little sneakers,
Four little, five little, six little sneakers,
Seven little, eight little, nine little sneakers,
Ten little purple sneakers.

How many sneakers?
Ten sneakers!

Ten little, nine little, eight little sneakers,
Seven little, six little, five little sneakers,
Four little, three little, two little sneakers,
One little purple sneaker.

How many sneakers?
One sneaker!

Practice.

How many cassettes?

Three cassettes.

1. 2. 3. 4. 5.

6. 7. 8. 9.

Learn the alphabet.

a b c d e f g h i j k l m n o p q r s t u v w x y z

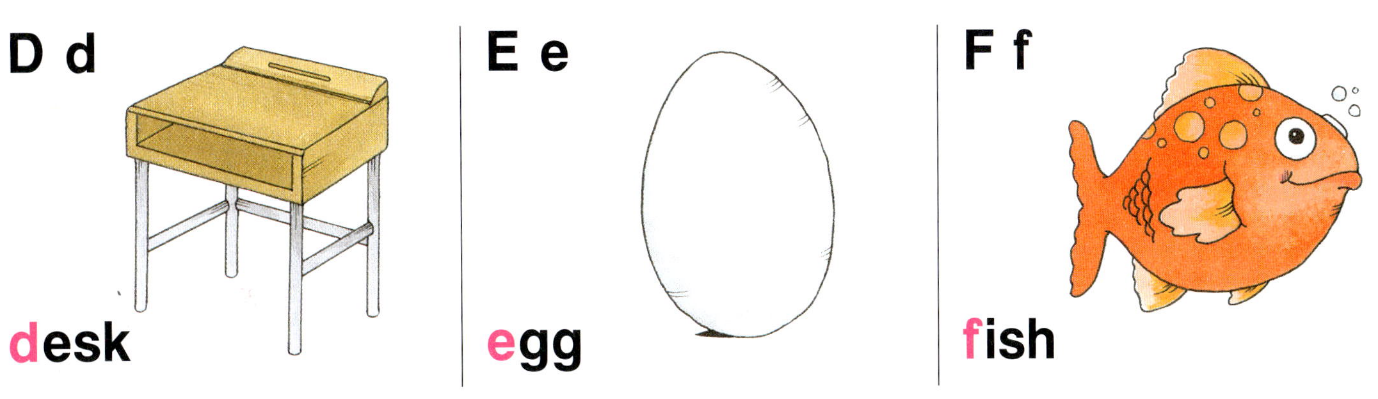

Let's Move

1. Make a circle.

2. Make two lines.

3. Go to the door.

4. Come here.

5. Count the girls.

6. Count the boys.

7. Draw a picture.

8. Give me the crayon.

Let's Listen

1.

2.

3.

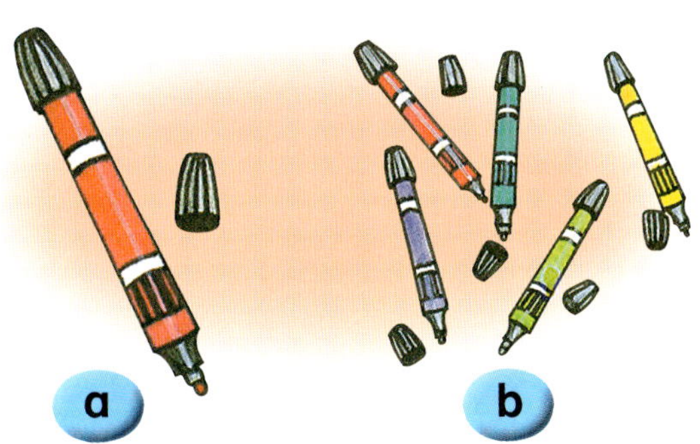

4.

5.

6.

7.

8.

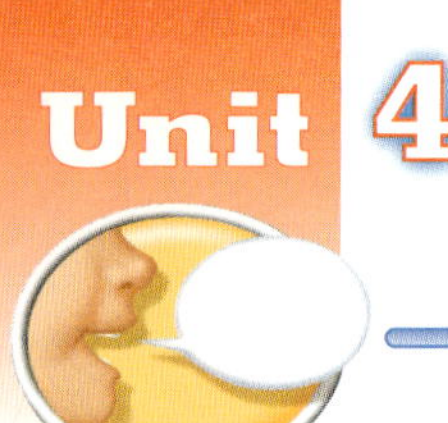

Let's Talk

It is nice to meet you.
It is nice to meet you, too.

It is = It's

Let's Sing

The Family Song

This is my mother.
Nice to meet you.
Nice to meet you, too.

This is my father.
Nice to meet you.
Nice to meet you, too.

This is my sister.
Nice to meet you.
Nice to meet you, too.

This is my brother.
Nice to meet you.
Nice to meet you, too.

Let's Learn

Who is she?
She is my grandmother.

Who is he?
He is my grandfather.

Who is = Who's
She is = She's
He is = He's

Ask your partner.

1. father
2. mother 
3. sister 
4. brother 
5. grandmother 
6. grandfather  
7. baby sister 
8. friend 

Who's he?

He's my father.

Say these.

Let's Learn Some More

He is tall.
She is short.

He is = He's
She is = She's

Practice.

He's young.

He's old.

1. young old
2. tall short
3. pretty ugly
4. thin fat

Guess.

1\.

She is old.
She is pretty.
Who is she?

She is my ________________.

2\.

She is pretty.
She is short.
Who is she?

She is my ________________.

3\.

He is tall.
He is thin.
Who is he?

He is my ________________.

4\.

She is young.
She is fat.
Who is she?

She is my ________________.

Learn the alphabet.

a b c d e f g h i j k l m n o p q r s t u v w x y z

G g	H h	I i	J j

girl	house	ink	jump rope

Let's Move

1. go to sleep 2. wake up 3. do homework 4. eat dinner

5. make a mess 6. clean up 7. watch TV 8. play the piano

Do not watch TV.

do not = don't

Don't watch TV.

Don't sit down.

Don't make a mess.

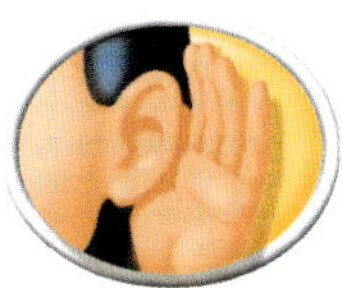

Let's Listen

1.

a

b

2.

a

b

3.

a

b

4.

a

b

5.

a

b

6.

a

b

7.

a

b

8.

a

b

Let's Review

A. Play a game.

B. Ask your partner.

Who's he?

He's my father. He's tall.

C. Say and act.

D. Answer the question.

How many _______?

E. Listen carefully.

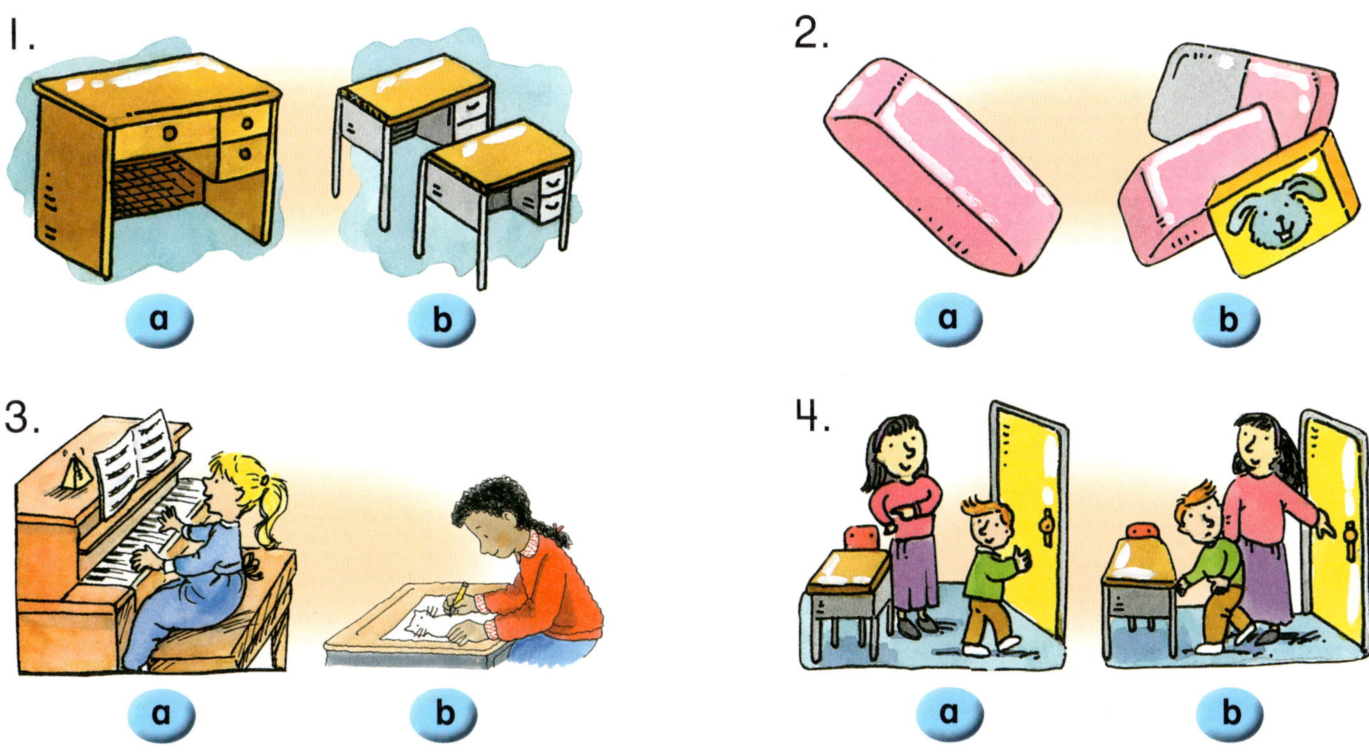

Unit 5

Let's Talk

How old are you?
I am seven years old.

I am = I'm

Let's Sing

The Happy Birthday Song

It's my birthday today.
It's your birthday today.
It's my birthday today.
Happy birthday, Jenny!

One, two, three, four, five, six,
Seven years old!

Now I'm seven years old.
Now you're seven years old.
Now I'm seven years old.
Happy birthday, Jenny!

Let's Learn

What is it?

I don't know.

What is it?

It's a doll.

What is it?
It is a doll.

It is = It's

Practice.

What is it?

It's a yo-yo.

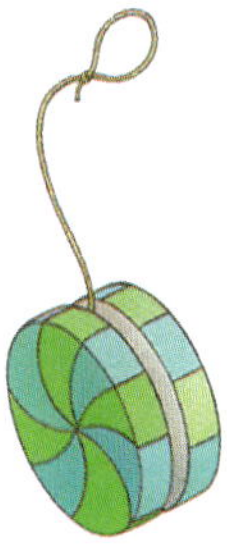

1. a yo-yo
2. a kite 
3. a car 
4. a ball 
5. a doll 
6. a puzzle 
7. a robot 
8. a jump rope 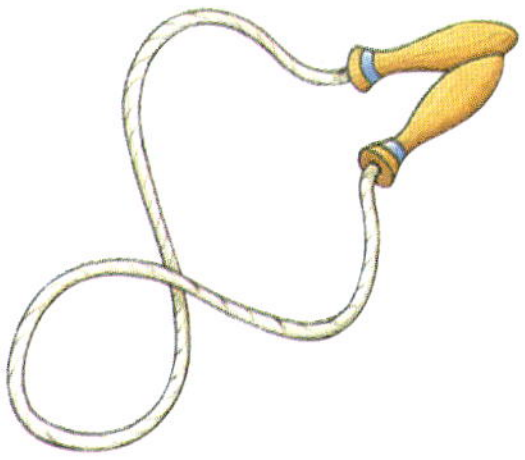
9. a bat 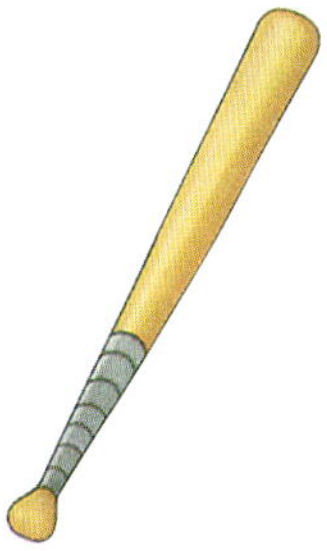
10. a bicycle 

Guess.

What is it?

Let's Learn Some More

It's little. What is it?

Is it a ball?

No, it isn't.

Is it a yo-yo?

Yes, it is.

It's a little yo-yo.

It is little.
It is a little yo-yo.

It is = It's

Say these.

Practice.

Is it a pencil?

Yes, it is. It's a long pencil.

Learn the alphabet.

a b c d e f g h i j **k l m n** o p q r s t u v w x y z

K k	L l	M m	N n
kite	**l**ion	**m**other	**n**otebook

Let's Move

1. play with a yo-yo

2. throw a ball

3. catch a ball

4. hit a ball

5. do a puzzle

6. jump rope

Can you play with a yo-yo?
Yes, I can.
No, I cannot.

cannot = can't

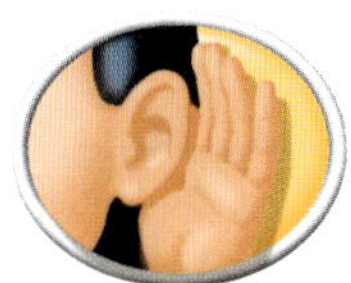

Let's Listen

1.

a b

2.

a b

3.

a b

4.

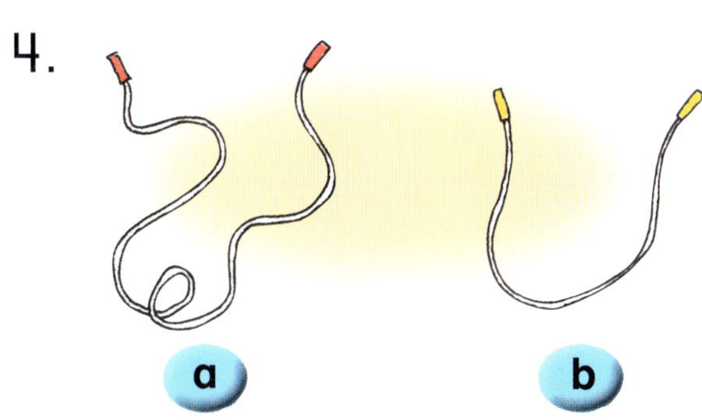

a b

5.

a b

6.

a b

7.

a b

8.

a b

Let's Talk

How is the weather?
It is sunny.

How is = How's
It is = It's

Let's Sing

How's the Weather?
How's the weather?
It's sunny.
How's the weather?
It's sunny.
How's the weather?
It's sunny. It's sunny today.
rainy
windy
cloudy
snowy

Let's Learn

How many clouds are there?

There are six clouds.

Oh, no! There's one big cloud!

How many clouds are there?
There are six clouds.
There is one cloud.

There is = There's

Practice.

Count them.

There is _____. There are _____.

Let's Learn Some More

Where's the kite?

It's in the tree.

Where are the books?

They're under the table.

Where is the kite?
It is in the tree.
Where are the books?
They are under the table.

Where is = Where's
It is = It's
They are = They're

Practice.

Where is the kite?

It's in the tree.

1. 2. 3. 4. 5. 6. 7. 8.

Learn the alphabet.

a b c d e f g h i j k l m n o p q r s t u v w x y z

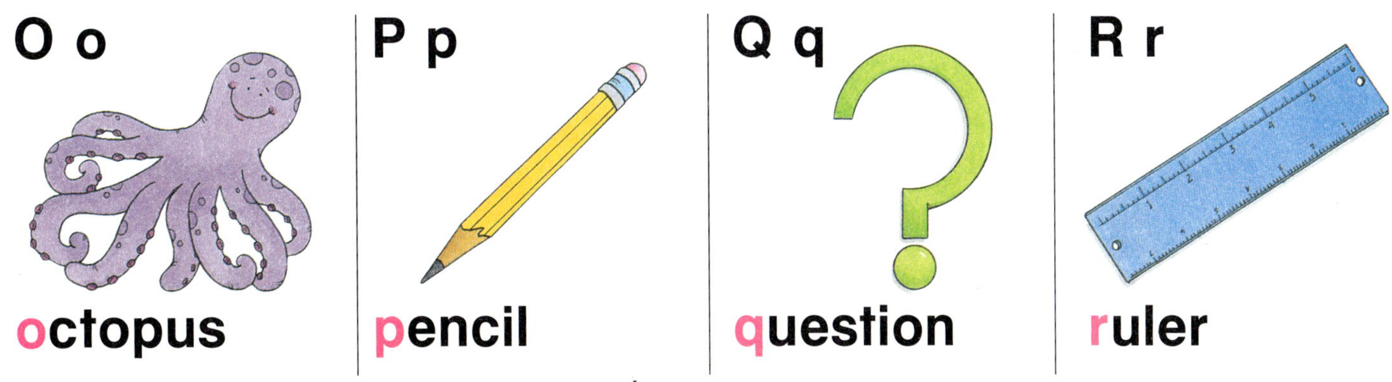

O o — octopus

P p — pencil

Q q — question

R r — ruler

Let's Move

1. climb a tree

2. play baseball

3. read a book

4. play tag

5. ride a bicycle

6. fly a kite

Can he climb a tree?
Yes, he can.
No, he cannot.

cannot = can't

Let's Listen

1.

2.

3.

4.

5.

6.

7.

8.
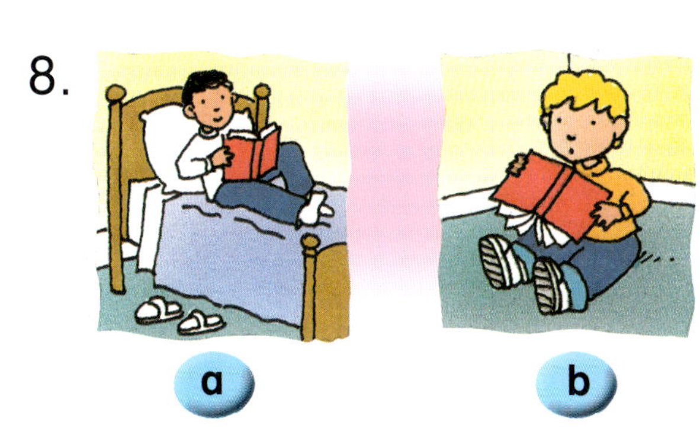

Let's Review

A. Play a game.

B. Answer the question.

How many _____ are there?

C. Say and act.

D. Ask your partner.

Can you _______?

Yes						
No						

E. Listen carefully.

Where is the cat?

1.

a b

2.

a b

3.

a b

4.

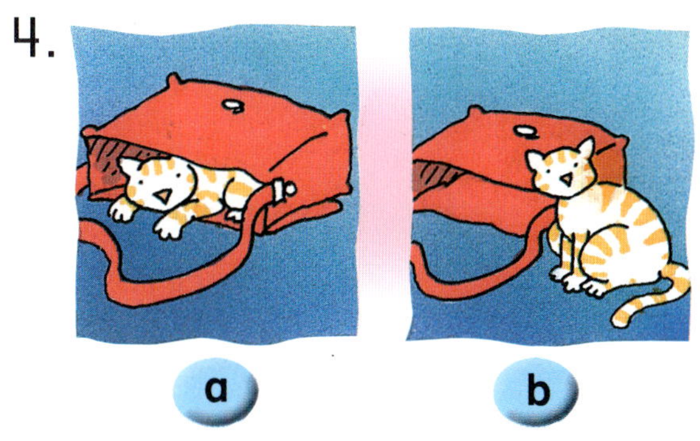

a b

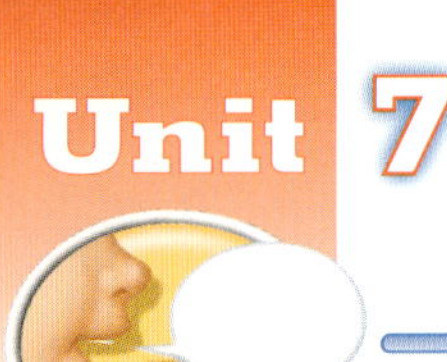

Let's Talk

Here you are.
Thank you.
You are welcome.

You are = You're

Let's Sing

Peaches, Apples, and Plums

Peaches, apples, and plums.
Peaches, apples, and plums.

What do you want?
I want an apple.

Peaches, apples, and plums.

Let's Learn

What do you want?

I want ice cream.

I want cake and ice cream.

Practice.

What do you want?

I want milk.

1. milk

2. fish

3. chicken

4. pizza

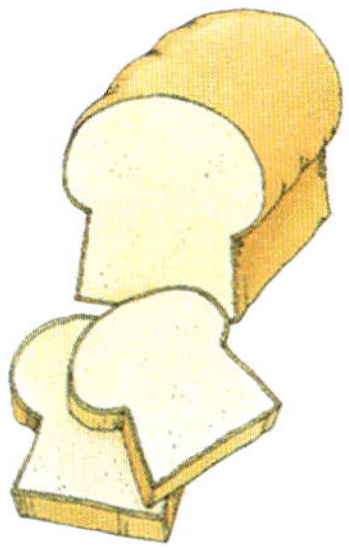

5. bread

6. rice

7. cake

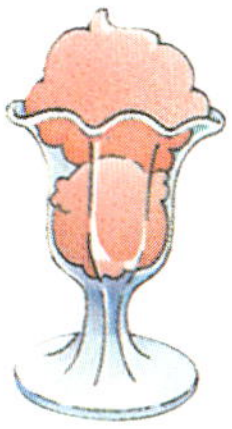

8. ice cream

Say these.

I want ______ and ______.

Let's Learn Some More

Do you want chicken?
Yes, I do.
No, I do not.

do not = don't

Do you want ice cream?

Yes, I do.

Practice.

1.

2.

3.

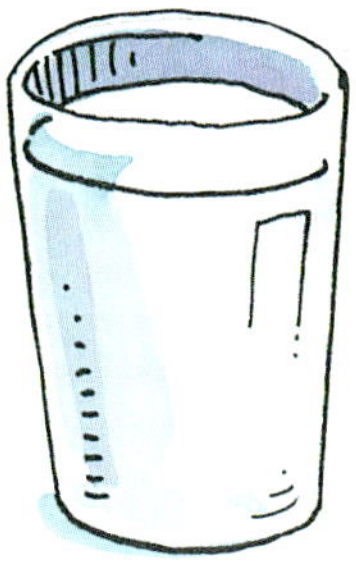

4.

5.

6.

7.

8.

Learn the alphabet.

a b c d e f g h i j k l m n o p q r s t u v w x y z

Let's Move

1\.

buy an apple	 wash it	 cut it	 eat it

2\.

buy juice	open it	pour it	 drink it

Answer the questions.

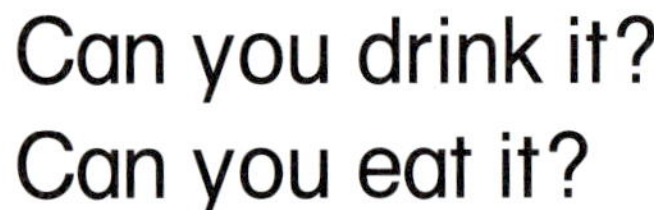

Can you drink it?
Can you eat it?

Let's Listen

1.

a b

2.

a b

3.

a b

4.

a b

5.

a b

6.

a b

7.

a b

8.

a b

Unit 8

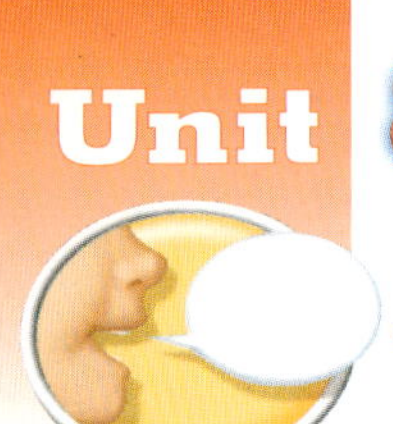

Let's Talk

What's your favorite color?

Red. What about you?

I like blue.

What is your favorite color?
Red.

What is = What's

Let's Sing

What Do You Like?

I like yellow, yes I do.
I like yellow, yes I do.
I like yellow.
    I do, too.
    I like yellow, too.

I like ice cream, yes I do.
I like ice cream, yes I do.
I like ice cream.
    I do, too.
    I like ice cream, too.

I like baseball, yes I do.
I like baseball, yes I do.
I like baseball.
    I do, too.
    I like baseball, too.

Let's Learn

Look! There's a dog. I like dogs.

What do you like?

I like frogs.

I like frogs, too.

What do you like?
I like frogs.
I like frogs, too.

Practice.

There's a bird. I like birds.

I like birds, too.

1. a bird — birds
2. a dog — dogs
3. a cat — cats
4. a frog — frogs 
5. a rabbit — rabbits
6. a spider — spiders

Ask your partner.

What do you like?

Let's Learn Some More

Do you like spiders?
Yes, I do.
No, I do not.

do not = don't

Practice.

Do you like robots?

No, I don't.

1.  2.  3.  4.  5.

6.  7.  8.  9.  10.

Learn the alphabet.

a b c d e f g h i j k l m n o p q r s t u v w x y z

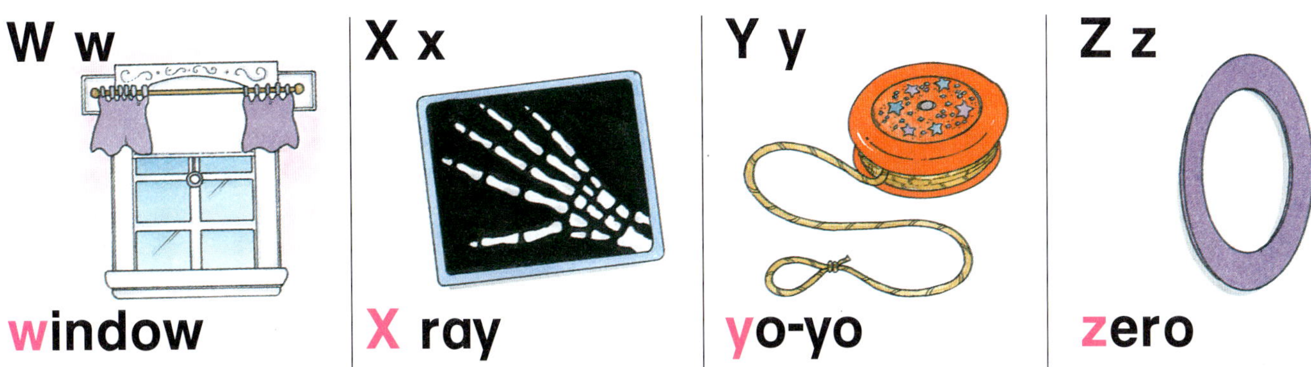

Let's Move

1. walk

2. run

3. swim

4. fly

5. hop

6. jump

Can it run?
Yes, it can.
No, it cannot.

cannot = can't

Answer the questions.

Can it run?
Can it hop?

Let's Listen

1.

a b

2.

a b

3.

a b

4.

a b

5.

a b

6.

a b

7.

a b

8.

a b

Let's Review

A. Play a game.

B. Answer the question.

Do you want ______?

C. Say and act.

D. Ask your partner.

Do you like ______?

Yes								
No								

E. Listen carefully.

1\.

a b

2\.

a b

3\.

a b

4\.

a b

Let's Go 1 Syllabus

UNIT	LANGUAGE ITEMS	FUNCTIONS	TOPICS
1	Hello, I am (Scott). Hi! My name is (Kate). What's your name? What's this? It's (a ruler). Is this (a book)? Yes, it is. No, it isn't.	Greetings Introducing yourself Asking someone's name Asking about objects (singular) Identifying objects (singular) Classroom commands	Names Classroom objects
2	How are you? I'm fine. Thank you. What color is this? It's (red)! This is a (blue) (book). This is a (red) and (yellow) book.	Greetings Asking about colors Identifying colors Describing objects Classroom commands	Colors Classroom objects
3	This is my friend, (Sarah). Hello, (Sarah). Let's play! What are these? They're (cassettes). How many (sneakers)? (Ten) (sneakers).	Introducing friends Suggesting an activity Asking about objects (plural) Identifying objects (plural) Asking about numbers Counting 1–10 Classroom commands	Numbers 1–10 Classroom objects
4	Hi, Mom! I'm home. This is my (mother). It's nice to meet you. It's nice to meet you, too. Who's (she)? (She's) my (grandmother). (She's) (short). Don't (watch TV).	Introducing family members Meeting someone politely Asking about people Identifying people Describing people Negative commands	Family
5	Happy birthday, (Jenny)! How old are you? I'm (seven) years old. This is for you. It's (my) birthday today. What is it? I don't know. It's (little). It's a (little) (yo-yo). Can you (play with a yo-yo)? Yes, I can. No, I can't.	Birthday greetings Asking and telling age Giving a gift Guessing Describing objects Asking about ability	Birthdays Age Toys

UNIT	LANGUAGE ITEMS	FUNCTIONS	TOPICS
6	How's the weather? It's (sunny). How many (clouds) are there? There are (six) (clouds). There's one (cloud). Where's the (kite)? It's (in) the tree. Where are the (books)? They're (under) the (table). Can (he) (climb a tree)? Yes, (he) can. No, (he) can't.	Asking about the weather Describing the weather Counting Describing a situation Asking about location Specifying location Asking about ability	Weather Outdoor activities
7	I'm (hungry). I want (an apple). Here you are. Thank you. You're welcome. What do you want? I want (cake) and (ice cream). Do you want (chicken)? Yes, I do. No, I don't. Buy (an apple). (Wash) it.	Expressing hunger and thirst Asking what someone wants Expressing wants Logical sequencing	Food and drink
8	What's your favorite color? (Red). What about you? I like (blue). What do you like? I like (frogs). I like (frogs), too. Do you like (spiders)? Yes, I do. No, I don't. Can it (run)? Yes, it can. No, it can't.	Asking about favorites Expressing likes Agreeing Asking about ability	Favorite colors Animals

Word List